MELLOWED BY TIME

By the same Author:

PRINTS AND IMPRESSIONS OF CHARLESTON

OTHER PLACES

Early Morning on Church Street

MELLOWED BY TIME

A Charleston Notebook

BY

ELIZABETH O'NEILL VERNER

Illustrated

With Pencil Drawings

by the Author

ꝰ

BOSTICK & THORNLEY, INC. • COLUMBIA, SOUTH CAROLINA

1953

First Printing, 1941

Second Printing, 1947

Third Printing, 1953

FOR

EMILY PERRY BROWN

WHO HAS ADOPTED US

AND WHOM

WE HAVE ADOPTED

ACKNOWLEDGMENTS

I would never have written this book at all if it had not been for

FANT THORNLEY *who believed I could do it, and* DR. CHAPMAN J. MILLING

who has been the most indulgent of critics.

ILLUSTRATIONS

MELLOWED BY TIME

MELLOWED BY TIME

A *Charleston Notebook*

&

Artists and historians are diametrically opposed in their approach to life. When an historian sees a spider web spun across a narrow walk from tree to wall, he unconsciously records that no one has passed that way for some time. He may be mistaken, however, for an artist may have preceded him and stopped to revel in the shimmering strands of light caught by the gossamer pattern and then walked around the fairy thing. But historians and artists are different. Now I am an artist and consequently this book is not an attempt at history. History deals in hard facts; it is all labelled with dates and pigeon-holed carefully, divided by wars and momentous political and social events. An historian is essentially a dealer in facts while the whole training of an artist is in the realm of fancy. To the artist the spirit rather than the letter is the important thing. Whatever else Charleston may be, she is different from any other city in America. This little notebook of mine attempts to tell wherein that difference lies. A library of historical data could never explain the charm of Charleston nor the passionate allegiance of her children.

I

A casual conversation I overheard not long ago was illuminating.

"For Lord's sake, where is you come from 'Becca, darlin'? I ain't know that you is in town; somebody is tell me you is gone Nort' to libe wid you daughter," a surprised voice said one morning on the narrow street just beyond my window. I glanced out and saw Rebecca push her cart, piled high with wilted produce, closer to the curb.

"I done bin gone and I come back," she said. "I don' like it up dere."

"Dat's so? Well I ain't gone away myself," said her friend, "so I don' know."

"You best stay right here where you is belong, sister," Rebecca advised. "Chas'n ain't no place for lebe. Seem like Chas'n keep all de odder place I see from seem natchel. I suits dis place cause it don't change none."

Off she trundled after this astute observation, but she left me thinking. It was easy to see that dear old simple Rebecca would not fit comfortably into a Harlem atmosphere, but wasn't it nice to think she could come home and find it had not changed!

Of course it had not changed! Rebecca could peddle her produce through the same streets, ring the same doorbells and sell her poor vegetables to the same families that she had known as a little barefoot girl when she came into town with her mother so long ago. She might expect the same bundles of old clothes and little presents of food and medicine; she could give an extra bunch of beets or carrots with a curtsey and feel a glow of self-respect; she, too, could give a present! She might weave a palmetto basket as a

2

Christmas gift and come home with her little cart piled high with goodies in return. These Charleston streets were the only life she knew, and they satisfied that craving for the continuity of human experience.

Rebecca crystallized my thoughts. I had been trying to define that peculiar charm which is Charleston's. Certainly nothing could be further apart than her viewpoint and my own, and yet she felt about Charleston very much as I did. That was what has always puzzled me; we all, every one of us, see a different Charleston and yet we are all in accord on this one point. There is no place like it in all the world!

I had it brought very forcibly to my attention some years ago that every one does not share our enthusiasm for Charleston. I was travelling in the Middle West at the time and was seated behind two salesmen. In the silence that followed the shriek of brakes as the train came to a sudden stop, their voices rang out clearly. There was no possibility that I had heard wrong. One man was saying, "But the worst town in these United States is Charleston, S. C. Ever been there?" I waited to hear this desecration violently rejected but all I heard from the other was, "You telling me!" The clamour of the starting train drowned their voices and although I strained my ears to listen, I could hear no more.

What had these two men experienced in this old city that I had fortunately missed? They had come to this small peninsula and found here the worst town in the United States!

So this little volume is not for them, nor is it for the young girl whom I met once in Georgia. She didn't like Charleston, either. She said there were too many goats in

Charleston. Now, I have never been troubled with goats in Charleston. I do remember one very famous goat, a goat none of us who crossed the street to avoid could have predicted would some day become immortal. Perhaps we would have looked twice at that little cart with the cripple had we known that Porgy was riding by. It would have seemed incredible to us that the pitiful creature huddled there would be selected as the fit subject for a masterpiece, that his name should be blazoned across Broadway and that he and his love affair should be put into an opera. Vividly I recalled him as I sat in that enthusiastic audience the opening night of *Porgy and Bess* in Boston. Never was there a sharper contrast—that poverty stricken derelict and the select gathering that had come to listen to his story. A poet had lifted that humble creature above his fellows and had given him immortality.

No, most of us would not even remember the goat or the man, except that our olfactory nerves were incensed, and olfactory nerves have long memories.

This little book is not for the travelling salesman, nor for the young girl who was annoyed with goats, nor for the tourist whom I once overheard saying to her friends, "Let's get out of this burg, it's dead!" It is for those who have seen a few of the same facets of the city that I have seen and for those who wish that they had. This is a goodly number; a most amazing number.

We must have something here; something that most of the world lacks today. Every time I drive down the old Meeting Street road, every time I cross the Ashley or Cooper rivers and enter the city, whether I come from the North,

4

The Huguenot Church

the West or the South, every time that feeling of rest comes over me; *I am at home.*

But even more I feel it when I glide in through the narrow channel at the jetties and see across the harbor the sky-line of the city with the gleam of St. Philip's cross, St. Michael's white spire, the copper domes of the old Scotch Church and far uptown the slender steeple of St. Matthew's, still our skyscrapers. What a world of heroism that narrow channel has witnessed, so close Fort Moultrie on one side and Fort Sumter on the other, and yet between these two a gap was once so wide that it split a nation. Such a very small city it is, compared to most cities, so confined by its rivers and harbor that it has been compressed and become an essence of itself.

It is impossible for me to enter Charleston from any side, whether by land or sea, and not feel that here the land is precious; here is a place worth keeping; this, of all the world, is home.

But others feel it, too, who are not at home in the sense that "home" means native land. Why do they, too, love it? Why do they say, "This is where I feel at home as nowhere else, this is where I would like to have been born, this is where I wish to end my days"?

No Charlestonian ever goes anywhere and says, "This is where I want to live; this is where I wish that I'd been born." Those who adopt us say they are from Charleston, but no Charlestonian ever says that he is from anywhere but Charleston, no matter where he lives nor how long he has lived there.

All over the world Charlestonians are scattered—exiles

from their native land. They come back at high moments—to be married, to bring out their daughters, to christen their grandchildren—it is the Mecca, the holy city.

But these others who choose us do not leave us to return to their native land for these great events. They marry their daughters in our churches, they give them balls in the Hibernian Hall, they adopt us whole-heartedly, and we take them in when they love Charleston. That seems to be the standard we have set for taking strangers in and making them at home. It is the only requisite. They must love the city as we love it to become one of us.

The only ones we never take in are those who have had to come and live here and who do not love the city. They stay lonely always. For that, and that only, is the unforgivable sin.

What has caused this deep-rooted devotion it is hard to define. Age and tradition are the obvious reasons, but it is more complex than that. It is true that the city is old, but not as old as Manhattan or Boston. It is true that it has traditions that have endured, though these have had to give way to the new order in other places equally as old, but it cannot be only age and tradition that make for this elusive something that I am trying to define. Too many whose roots were transplanted here, as were my own, share this passion for the city. Three generations is too short a time to have lived here to count, if tradition be the only criterion.

One bitter cold January day I was waiting at the Pennsylvania station in New York for my train home. When I told the Red Cap who had grabbed my bag that I wanted the train to Charleston, his ebony features broke into a

The Lesesne Gates

smile, and a flash of white split his mouth from ear to ear. "Chas'n, missus? Please ma'm, you set right here 'til I come back. I gwine to git de Chas'n boys." With that the news spread, and the Red Caps on nimble legs started gathering. Across from me sat an exceedingly well-groomed woman with all the earmarks of a seasoned traveller. She listened with amazement to our conversation. An impromptu party had sprung up before her. "How very strange!", her eyebrows said. Surrounded by Red Caps I was given messages to bring home.

"Missus, you know my brudder, he wuk to de Liberty Cleanin' Company; if you is see um, please ma'm tell um I comin' home on my holiday." With just pride another announced that his father was the only colored member of the police "fose." All wanted to go home. There was a friendly scuffle as to who would carry my bags; a crowd started to gather. I was very embarrassed.

One of them boasted proudly, "Dis ain' nothin', missus, to de Grand Central station; de head Red Cap of all is Poinsett to de Grand Central. If you goes there, just say 'Chas'n' and you watch dem boys step 'cause de big boss of all de whole crowd is Poinsett of Chas'n."

I looked up; the Christmas decorations were still in the station. I wondered if the great Joel R. Poinsett, for whom the scarlet-pointed flower was named, would not have been happy to know that one Poinsett would some day be in the exalted position of head Red Cap at the Grand Central station in the world's great metropolis bestowing hospitality upon stray Charlestonians.

Charleston is more than a city. This intense local patriotism gives the little strip of land a national dignity.

When my daughter was living in Cambridge, I unselfishly released my claim on Willie; there seemed nothing else to do. I was utterly bereft. I lost an amateur painter, gardener, model, butler and cook. I lost also a five-piece band under one management, for Willie was all of that. With the assistance of a washboard, a fork and a mouth organ to which a tomato can had been attached in some miraculous way, and a right foot which directed, he was the delight of all my young neighbors and a social asset very few are favored with.

Think of owning a band that can clean windows, wash cars, paint the bathroom, mend the hose and bow company in and out with an irresistible smile!

More for his sake than my own, however, I dreaded to see him go. He would be homesick; he would not like Cambridge. A yearning to have my small grandson tenderly cared for by his gentle hands; to have his baby feet tap time to "Dat Ole Time Religion;" to know that my daughter would never have one anxious moment when she trusted the baby to his care, at last won me over to buying the ticket and sending him forth to parts unknown.

What was my dismay on returning home to find a telegram from my young family, "Better not send Willie, can find no place for him to live in Cambridge." Well, it was too late now. It was out of my hands, but I was not happy about it.

I was so unhappy about it that I jumped in my car and decided to see for myself how things were going. So, unannounced, I arrived a few days later in Cambridge.

The front door yielded in the little apartment on Brattle

Street, and I slipped in quietly. Back I went through the long hall to the pantry. Seated in a high chair was my grandson, his eyes shining with delight, and leaning over him, spoon in hand, was Willie. But it was his voice, those deep organ notes, that made my throat tense.

"Buh Turkey laff right in Buh Buzzard face," he was telling the little boy. "You *got* for laff at Buh Buzzard, ef you wanta beat um, 'cause Buh Buzzard, him jest natcherly don' know how for laff."

"William, you're all right?" I asked him later. "You're happy up here?"

"Yas ma'm, missus, I'se happy *now*; I ain' been happy at fust, but now I is," he said, beaming, "cause I find a place to stay dat suit me. You is know the Warley family ob Chas'n, ain' you, missus?" he asked me anxiously. It was very important to him that I should know them. Fortunately, I could assure him that they were my friends.

"Well," he said, relieved, "I's stay'n wid de colored branch ob de Warley fam'ly in Cambridge. Dey say I kin stay wid dem if I brings dem de *News and Courier* every evening when I comes from wuk."

I found that the "colored branch of the Warley family" had lived in Cambridge for sixteen years! Even we who were merely friends of the white branch felt a certain social security. The *News and Courier* every day was a rock we could all rally around and from it gain solace in that different world.

The little apartment in Cambridge became a magnet to the Charleston boys at Harvard. They would come in homesick and leave refreshed. I remember one young fellow particularly. It was his first experience so far away from home, and he was a good story teller, as the majority of Charlestonians are, and delighted in the vagaries of the Negro. He had a ready audience; we would gather around and listen. Just before he had left home he had gone down with some friends to a plantation. It was hot and humid. The owner of the place had said to his faithful caretaker, "Well, Jim, I hope you are sleeping better now that you have your mosquito net."

Jim scratched his head and shuffled his feet. "Boss, I sorry, but dat net you is brought me ain't no good; I cas' 'em and cas' 'em, but I ain't catch no skeeter yet."

The story brought a familiar picture to them all. The long avenue with dripping moss, the quiet country, the simple people whom they loved, did not seem so far away.

In the far corners of the world these meetings take place. An immediate bond is found, race and class are unimportant, when the discovery is made that Charlestonian is meeting Charlestonian. I never tired of hearing my father tell of detecting the sound of a Charleston voice in a Paris restaurant as a boy. For four long years he had not heard that particular cadence. It was to him what Hawaiian music is to the *kamaaina*—irresistible.

There is something in the pitch of our voices, whether cultivated or the reverse, that is recognizable. Wherever we go—we are marked. It would be difficult for a Charlestonian to travel incognito. Our voices are pitched lower, there is a cover tone, our pronunciation of the vowels "e" and "a" exasperate telephone operators elsewhere, and there is a certain twist to our "c's" and "g's" which gives those

14

The Miles Brewton House

consonants a different sound in such words as *girl, car* and *garden.*

Many years ago when travel was not as common as it is today, a young Savannah lawyer went down to breakfast in a hotel in Hong Kong. A gentleman came forward and greeted him. "The *gyarden* here is very beautiful," he said, "may I have the pleasure of showing it to you?"

The young man from Savannah grasped his hand. "Why you're an *Overhomer*," Mr. Walter Hartridge exclaimed. Now "over home" means only one thing in Savannah, and an Overhomer is a Charlestonian. "Yes, my name is Gaillard, and I am from Charleston; when did you leave Savannah," the other asked without further explanation.

On the other side of the globe they had met, but had it been on Mars it would have been the same. By one word from each — *Overhomer* and *Garden* — they had placed one another.

I have heard stories of reunions on the Trans-Siberian railway, in the jungles of South America and in Alaska. Whenever they meet it is the same. They find refreshment and comfort in just knowing that here is another who has smelled the pluff mud, walked the narrow streets and watched the gulls flutter over the high Battery wall.

More real than brick and mortar is this intangible bond. Elusive perhaps, hard to define, but so potent that travel where they may Charleston holds her children, native born and adopted, with ropes so strong that no place on earth ever quite anchors them when once they have called the city *home.*

17

Two young men from the North visited Charleston many years ago. They fell in love with the city and they made a pact. When they could, they would retire here. The years rolled around. Each was gaining reputation, power and prestige in his separate calling. Both succeeded beyond the dreams of most, and then they met in Charleston to live. They are here now, having bought homes that they have enhanced in beauty. They enter into our civic and social life and have attracted many of their friends from distant states. They have seen so many places in their active lives, and they could live anywhere they wished. What was it in this quiet city that had gripped their young imaginations so that they never forgot that youthful pact? What vision of a better way of living? Was it that here they hoped to find again the feeling of home, which in their childhood could be found in many places in America? They weren't seeking Charleston in their latter years because it was different; they were seeking it because it was strangely familiar.

All around us are friends who have stopped for a casual visit and are staying for life. Here they have found the haven they were seeking. In most places today the people are striving to live, and here we are living. Here we are rich without effort in the priceless things too dear to buy. When a man acquires wealth he first tries to buy leisure. Leisure—such a beautiful word—a sort of glorified wealth in time. One of the most pathetic paradoxes life holds is our strenuous American business man trying to buy leisure. He goes so violently about it with his yachts, plantations, golf and shooting that he is likely to die of heart disease or exhaustion before he discovers that the commodity is not purchasable with money at all.

Most Americans are poor in time. They have to spend so much of it in the machinery of living. Suburban trains, subways, congested traffic, dentist's appointments, shopping —all these things so waste it that there is little time left to live in.

Charleston has a wealth of time. The days are long because the distances are short. No driving twenty miles or so to lunch with a friend; the chances are your best friend is your closest neighbor, or at most lives a block away. There is plenty of time to visit, to gossip, to read or walk. Long blank spaces with "no instant need of things" to be done.

Broad street any morning of the week resembles a gentleman's club. Gathered in doorways out of the sun the men stand and talk and, better still, laugh. They tell their wives that they do business that way. They probably do, but where else on earth is business done that way, I ask you? They have time between deals to enjoy themselves. They scarcely need the yacht clubs or the many Charleston clubs. Just a stroll through the streets gives them a moving party, so to speak.

If by chance you feel lonely in Charleston, just put on your hat and walk around the block. You will meet many a friend on that walk. Each will have time to converse with you, and you will come home refreshed.

This may all sound very provincial; the same might be said of any small town in America, but the difference is that Charleston hasn't been a small town for over two hundred years.

It has long been a city and has very few of the characteristics of a small town. In that walk around the block, you

19

might perhaps meet five or more people who are nationally known and a great number more who should be. You will get a dozen different opinions on vital local and international questions; you will meet persons who have travelled and are well-informed. You will meet no rustic philosopher on that walk, charming though it might be to meet one. You will probably converse with as sophisticated a company as is to be met with anywhere in the world in so small a space, unless, perchance, you happen upon a friend of the darker race, which will be equally diverting. A flower woman, perhaps, swinging rhythmically along, both arms free, and on her head a fanner basket laden with the glory of the season, some way, somehow, arranged unconsciously by artist's hands. She may persuade you to buy in spite of the fact that your house is already laden with flowers by telling you that she "ain't made but fi'teen cent today and I done eat dat up."

If you encourage her by your sympathy the least bit, she may elaborate on her plight, "And I ain't got no eensurance, neither, missus; and I feel the misery comin' on."

You are shocked at such slipshod living.

"No insurance," you exclaim; "why I thought you had insurance, Josie; you used to carry it. Why did you give it up?"

"Well, missus," Josie may say to you, "I gi' 'em up 'cause I find dat de hand dat I done gee' de money to is leak." And then you come home from your walk with no loose change in your purse!

Although Charleston is urban in every sense of the word it is singularly free from pretense, for there is no one

Gates of the Charleston Free Library

to impress. We are what we are. We are as old as we are, certainly, and, since age imparts distinction, it would be foolish to hide such an asset. We are as clever or as dull as we are; too many schoolmates around to fake on that either. We are as rich or as poor as we are; no use to pretend the one nor to hide behind the other. If we are rich, we can give larger donations to charity, have bigger parties, wear more expensive clothes, drive larger cars, but we can have no better friends, for most of us are not rich—not even what elsewhere might be considered comfortable. We are comfortable in Charleston, however, since money is no standard.

Long has the city known what many parts of the country only began to understand ten years ago. The discipline of seventy-five years of not being able to buy pleasure has developed our capacity to enjoy to the full the things that are not bartered in the market place. Happiness simply has nothing to do with money at all.

Poverty and want may not have touched us personally, but their cruel fangs have made unforgettable scars on those we love and we have seen the scars. A cherished old lady, exquisitely dressed, surrounded by every comfort, told me a story once that I have never forgotten. We were sitting on her piazza; through the points of the palmetto a shimmer of the waters of the harbor was visible; tiny white sails broke the blue from time to time; it was all so peaceful—so comfortable.

A gentle breeze brought to our nostrils the faint aroma of cooking yams from a neighbor's kitchen, those juicy tubers that ooze golden sweetness. She caught the odor and instantly it brought back a picture of long ago which she painted for me so graphically that I shall see it always.

During the bombardment of Charleston every town and city in South Carolina opened its doors to fleeing Charlestonians. There is not a Charleston family that does not have in its heart an especial love for some town in upper Carolina. My friend's family refugeed in Aiken. She was one of many children. No men accompanied these refugees; a faithful servant or two and a valiant band of women, mothers, aunts, and perhaps a grandmother, went forth into a strange new world armed with nothing but their fearless spirits and standards of life held high above material things. These they would hand on to their children inviolate.

Since corn pone and molasses are irksome food, there was great jubilation among the children when one morning a present of a basket of yams was sent over with the compliments of the head mistress of a seminary for young ladies. These young ladies were the exiles' closest neighbors and friends in their new home. All day long the children begged for the yams, but their mother thought they would sleep if they had them for supper. For many a night they had been restless for lack of sufficient food. When at last the potatoes were placed in the ashes on the hearth, the excitement was high. A whole yam apiece! They could hardly wait! More and more tempting the tubers became as the juice oozed out and the mellifluent odor filled the room. Even now, after seventy years, my old friend remembered that aroma.

Just as the great moment came and a long fork had tested the golden joys and found them done to a turn, there were heard outside shrill giggles and a clamor which had an

The Villa Margherita

ominous sound to the hungry little band. The seminary girls were coming for a visit! In they bounced, all unconscious of the tragedy they were causing.

"My, those yams smell good!" they said. "Yes, they do; you are just in time to share them with us," said the Spartan mother. Not even a look was necessary to curb her children; well they knew the code. Another night of gnawing hunger was far less an evil than lack of hospitality.

Because we have lived in the shadow of want and seen poverty at close range, it is rather difficult to impress us with exterior things. Our sense of values is well balanced. We have found from experience that life plays strange pranks and likely as not, bestows her greatest blessings, contentment and serenity, with a lavish hand on the one we would pity, and often gives but grudgingly to the one we had been disposed to envy. We see such startling contrasts all about us.

One day I sat for hours in the company of a flower woman in tattered coat covering layers of dresses, holding in her hand a pitiful bunch of jonquils wrapped in moss. Such tiny, wilted jonquils, hardly recognizable as such, but all that she had to bring to town that day. It took more skill than I possessed to paint the flowers as she hoped they would be. I heard tales of poverty that were hard to credit, but I knew that they were true, for I had visited her cabin. I had seen the patch of hard ground just outside the shanty with its clay chimney, sufficiently askew to suit a cubist's canvas.

Had I not known her so well I would have been wrung with pity over her poverty. It was useless to pity her, however. The face which I was trying to paint was carved deep around eyes and mouth with lines of contentment. She had not complained; she seemed perfectly happy. Perhaps she was really richer, after all, than the woman I dined with later, for in the evening of the same day I found no withered jonquils! Orchids—not ordinary orchids, either, but rare specimens, named for members of her family, propagated in her own greenhouse and shipped in fresh every day or so. Not just a few orchids, but orchids everywhere, and everything else that goes with orchids. And I learned that peace, serenity and contentment are not necessarily cultivated with orchids!

Since there is nobody to impress, we do as we please, work when we need to work at anything we find at hand to do, being sure that no matter what it is, we will not lose face with our friends. If we have enough, we do not work, being sure, too, that we will not be criticized as loafers. We play together—those who work and those who do not, and the one thing we all know how to do is to play.

❧

When I was a child, my grandfather on very special occasions would let me play with a series of Italian paintings of rural scenes which he treasured greatly. These were on thin wood, and there were twenty-four of them in all. Each panel was about six inches wide and ten inches long. Strung together in the order in which they were numbered, they made a most fascinating Italian landscape. The magic of them, however, lay in the fact that each scene so completely fit every other scene that they could be arranged in any manner and still the effect would be perfect. Charleston's social life has always reminded me of the joy I found in trying out these pictures in strange combinations. There are many little groups in Charleston that are entirely complete within themselves, but combine each of them with any other group and the result is unexpectedly delightful.

Never have I been to a dull party in Charleston. No matter what the combination of guests, young or old or very young, it is always the same, a perfect party, the best ever! Each guest seems as responsible as the hostess; it is the thing Charleston does best of all—give a party. Nowhere else do gaiety and dignity blend with such perfect harmony. Differences are left at the door; they can be settled somewhere else; the party is the thing. No cliques, no men gathered in one corner and women in another; the throng is mobile, it moves easily; all seem glad to be here, all go away refreshed. We never hire entertainers nor plan amusements; just meeting each other seems pleasure enough to most of us. Drinking is never discussed; one drinks or not; it is left to the individual. To drink too much, however, is the social sin seldom forgiven.

History will tell you that we have a record as a hotheaded city. We are still hot-headed. Almost always we have an issue to settle. We are not timid. We disagree violently with our best friends. We hold meetings and express our opinions with oratory worthy of Calhoun or Hayne. There is little monotony. It is too bad to be away long at a time. So much happens when one is away!

And with it all, we do not change as other cities change. Coming back after twenty years, we hear Charlestonians say, "It is just the same." We live in the same houses for the most part. Charlestonians hate to move; moving is a calamity. Moving means uprooting and change—our roots are deep—we do not like to change.

As I have said before, we all see things differently. This book just happens to express the way I see it. The sharp individuality developed through our ease of living and our geographical isolation breeds many opinions. I think it is a tribute to our humanity and a measure of our moderation to remember that Charleston has never paid greater honor to any one of her children in all her long history than she has paid to James L. Petigru. He was a son adopted, not native-born, who boldly dared to disagree with public opinion in Charleston's greatest crisis, and there is no record of her past she more proudly shows the visitor than the classic epitaph in St. Michael's churchyard recording that act of courage—

> He withstood his People for his Country
> But his People did homage to the Man
> Who held his conscience higher than their praise
> And his Country
> Heaped her honours on the grave of the Patriot
> To whom, living
> His own righteous self-respect sufficed
> Alike for Motive and Reward.

It is said that Woodrow Wilson, while at the Versailles Conference, cabled to Charleston for a copy of this epitaph.

In Charleston as elsewhere none of us really knows what another sees or feels; we have only words to attempt to convey our impressions, and words are so faulty a medium. What to me may be beauty, to another may have no beauty at all; what to me may be a tribute worth braving

Charleston Water-front

the whole world to be worthy of, may to another, be a tombstone in a quiet graveyard and nothing more.

❧

That reminds me of an incident that brought forcibly home to me how very differently two people may react to the same event. A bridge was to be opened which was an important link in the highway leading into Charleston. Most of the city was attending the celebration. Two friends asked me to go, but for some forgotten reason, I could not. The next day one friend came in to tell me how very sorry she was that I was not with her. "Never in my life have I seen anything lovelier; I don't know what it was, but the atmosphere had a glow about it that was most unreal. The trees became a flat pattern of silver against a sky of gold; it had the appearance of a glorified block-print. I longed for you all day," she said.

Some hours later the other friend dropped in. "My dear," she exclaimed, "how lucky you were to have stayed at home. Yesterday was terrific! Never did I see such dust; it simply filled the air; one could hardly breathe. Much as we missed you, I'm glad you were spared the ordeal!"

But I was not glad that I had missed the day. I would have seen the glorified block-print of silver and gold even though I knew the illusion was caused by the same dust that was choking me.

❧

I see our Negroes as an integral part of the beauty of Charleston. Their faces vary as much as our own, and their shining dark skins reflect many colors. Their bodies under

33

their clothes have unconscious grace. For this reason I never pose a model. I wait until they fall naturally into a position I want, and then work swiftly, very swiftly, for they never again quite repeat the pose.

If Maggie had not been utterly picturesque I would not have been so persistent in my appeal that she pose for me. At last she consented to stand, basket on head, in my garden for a very short time at a very large price. She stood stiff as a ramrod, hands folded across her spacious bosom, head erect, feet firmly planted. I could do nothing, and the time was slipping by. Strategy was necessary.

"How many children have you got, Maggie?" I casually inquired.

"Chillun? Well le' me see, Missus," she said, relaxing every line as she slipped her weight on one foot and rested her hand on her ample hip.

I drew swiftly. A dreamy look came into her eyes; she was thinking, and slowly she began to count aloud.

"I got t'ree head, and" (after a pause) "den I got t'ree mo'" —(another pause). "You know dat flues dat everybody is git sick wid after de war; well I was real lucky wid dat flues. I only lost two head of my chillun at dat time," she boasted proudly.

"Then," I said, "you have four children left, haven't you, if you had three and then three and lost two?"

"No, ma'm, I has a heap more dan dem fust two set. I has Joe (him as cuts de wood), and Dora and Ileen and Ca'line and dem leetle ones dat ain't beyant knee age."

"My gracious," I exclaimed, "you surely have got a lot of children! I hope you have a good husband to help you take care of them."

34

The pose was lovely now; every line relaxed. I was quite excited over my progress, but I had gone a step too far and my hopes were shattered in the twinkling of an eye, for Maggie was instantly rigid with righteous wrath, and my pose was gone forever.

"Who? Me have husband! No ma'm, Missus, I ain't got no husband and never did had. I ain't want no good for nothin' man hangin' round my house. Dem is my own chillun; every blessed one of dem belongs to me!"

❧

I think people have time to remember better in Charleston than in most places. Perhaps it is easier to remember here where the generations are all known to each other and linked up, for by the time one has reached the half-century mark, a Charlestonian is likely to have known five generations of any family. Watching a little child trudging down to the Battery with his baby fingers clutching trustingly the brown-veined hands of his nurse, it is interesting to speculate upon the future of that child. Will he inherit from this line or that? Most likely you know them all. He is not just a baby to you, but a friend in embryo. You know so many things about him that he will never know about himself! One old lady of eighty told one, with all sincerity, that it was time for her to die; she remembered too much.

Some of the nicest things I know about Charleston have been told to me by old ladies. We have always had a lot of them, and when an old house was being torn down some years ago, a wag announced that he bet the old ladies would run out of it like ants. We revere them and grieve when we lose them, for old ladies seem to have gone out of style in most places. Elderly women appear to be taking their places. I like old ladies best—the ones with caps.

The reverence with which Charleston has always regarded her old ladies once caused me great embarrassment. Some years ago for a fancy dress ball, I decided to make up as an old Charleston lady. It was an easy costume to assemble; I was offered innumerable black silk dresses with dainty white collars and cuffs, and a friend lent me an exquisite cap of her grandmother's. My hair was powdered and "parallel lines delved in beauty's brow"—to say nothing of cheek and chin. The make-up was all too convincing. Consternation greeted me as I walked in; sobriety and deference surrounded me all evening. After a startled glance I was recognized, but that did not seem to help the situation much for—I——wore——the——cloth! Pirates and Confederates reverently kissed my hand. Not one asked me to dance! Not that our old ladies do not dance at the coming-out parties of their granddaughters, but gentlewomen do not appear in assemblages with peasant girls, Pierrots and pirates.

When I wanted to make an etching of the Sword Gates from the inside some years ago, one of these ladies demonstrated to me how memories of the past persist. It never occurred to me that it would be difficult for me to make an etching from the garden walk. All my life I had lived within a stone's throw of the Sword Gates, and I had painted them even as a child, sitting on a neighbor's step opposite, but the Sword Gates were beginning to attract attention, and the family who owned and lived in the house

36

St. Michael's Spire over Roof Tops

was considerably annoyed by the constant ringing of the bell and requests from so many strangers to let them enter the garden. They had been forced to lock the gate and instruct their servants to deny requests for entrance, except to persons known to the family.

I rang with no premonition that I was tackling a difficult task. Slowly down the long flagged walk, solemn with deep shadows from the magnolia trees overhead, a woman came to answer the bell. Giving her my name I asked her to go to her mistress and tell her that I would like permission to draw in her garden. She did not recognize my name and "to draw in the garden" had the sound she suspected.

"No ma'm, you can't come in," she said, firmly, "and I can't ask she; she don't wanta be disturved; she don't want nobody to draw in de gyarden."

"Will you please go and ask her," I insisted.

The argument was long, but in the end I won with a note of command that she recognized as "belonging." Slowly she dragged her weight up the path to the house. Her feet seemed leaden. In less time than seemed possible, she was skipping back, her face a broad grin. The key was quickly turned, and with a deep curtsey, she opened the heavy iron gate.

"You come right in, ma'm, and I'll bring you a chair. My missus say to tell you dat you is mos' welcome and dat she is comin' right down to see you herself."

The transition was so sudden that I was puzzled. I had been sure before I asked that my request to enter the garden would be granted, but why this exceeding cordiality? I could not understand. I knew so well from experience that our servants are all mimics, reflecting our moods, our prejudices, and adopting unquestioningly our friends. But this lady I did not know by sight, strange as that may seem, being such a close neighbor. She knew *of* me, however. To her I was not just a Charleston artist who happened to be her neighbor. I was very much more than that. I was the great-granddaughter of Mary Ann Harrison, who had saved her distinguished father's life when he was in prison during the war!

I had never heard the story until then, and she would never have had occasion to tell it, except that after seventy years the time had come for her to open a gate to me that would have been closed to a stranger. All over Charleston are such stories.

I was told only a few months ago by a Charleston woman that when my father was in the Charleston Light Dragoons, he had saved her uncle's life in the bitter riots of '76. Both these bits of past family history impressed me —not because they were about my people, who have lived here a comparatively short time, but because I feel sure that they *are* typical cases. Think of the wealth of such anecdotes to be gathered concerning families who have been living here for well over two hundred years, and the intimacy and cohesion of a group so inter-connected.

❧

I wish I knew all about the Sword Gates, for every day during the tourist season I am asked about them. I recall remembering them at the Old Guard House, where the post-office now stands. I feel sure they had flat sheets of iron back of them at that time. I have always heard that they

A Wrought Iron Gateway

were made in Charleston, and fantastic stories about Madame Talvande's building the high wall and moving the gates there when the Old Guard House was torn down, because one of the young ladies of her seminary had eloped. I advise you to look this up elsewhere, if you really want to know—I don't—for to me they are very especially my gates, as I saw with my own eyes fairies in the garden as I peered through them while walking down with my nurse to the Battery. That was really why I wanted to draw them from the inside, if you wish to know the truth.

❧

I have said that our servants are mimics; they are. Often I mistake over the phone the voice of her servant for the voice of a friend, but it is equally true that unconsciously we mimic them. The pitch of our voices is settled before we talk at all, and I hope very much that my black *Dah* had something to do with mine. Their graphic way of speech is such a constant delight to us that no doubt we have been affected by it.

What could be more descriptive than my Dilsie's account of a traffic accident, "When I was comin' to wuk dis mawnin', I is see two cars is come to a conclusion."

"She tie me for loose she," is so much more graphic than "She's the culprit and she's throwing the blame on me to distract your mind from herself." What criticism of a portrait more graphic than "Dat is sure a sad resemblance of Mr. Dan."

Nothing amuses us more than to pass on these absurdities. All of us do it, but few are guilty of keeping an inefficient servant for seven years as I did, because I enjoyed listening to her talk. Nothing that I have ever seen or heard, on the stage or off, remotely approached Dilsie in dramatics. The roll of her eyes, the toss of her head, the infinite inflections of her voice, her choice of words and her philosophy all delighted me. Her conscience was as under-developed as her histrionics were the reverse.

One morning I heard, "I ain' gonna buy no mo' shrimp fum you; you is scant de plate on me too much," from Dilsie; and an indignant gruff protest, "I ain' scant de plate on you; dat is a full plate."

"Yes, you is, too. Dat ain' no shrimp to what I gets from my cousin Sammy."

A deep grumble, a pause and a pleased murmur, and I could imagine the pantomime going on on my front steps. "Now dat's a whole lot better! Well, good mawnin'!" in cat-licked-cream tones from Dilsie.

"Why don't you buy from your cousin Sammy if he gives you so many shrimp?" I asked later. We are all very fond of shrimp for breakfast.

"Do Lawd! missus," Dilsie laughed at my innocence. "I ain' got no cousin Sammy; I just tell um dat to get de broadus."

Her speaking voice had to be checked and controlled for so small a house as ours, but her singing voice was pure, vibrant music. She complained of it, though. She would become unhappy when she was singing alone in the kitchen because the Lord only gave her one throat.

"It ain' no sport fuh sing with jest one trote," she would say; "You got for have t'ree trotes fuh sing good!" I was quite struck with the idea myself. It would be lots of fun to sing close harmony alone!

She quoted the Bible to her purpose. The earth was the Lord's, not her landlord's, who protested that she dug too many holes in his yard, filling tomato cans for her "gereeniums."

"De land is his'n but the earth is de Lord's, and I is He child and I know He ain' gwine to deny me dat little bit ob earth fo' my po' little flowers." Again I thought that fair. Surely she should have that handful of trampled dust. I was too familiar with the results not to feel that the Lord was indeed with her in this. Drab little window ledges jewelled with bloom are a common sight in Charleston.

But when she would not keep the screen door of the kitchen shut and I warned her that if she let the flies come in they would give us the typhoid fever, I could not see things her way. She was indignant that I should attribute to a fly the power which was clearly the Lord's. She'd keep the screen door shut because she was told to do so, but her motive would be obedience to an order. Then her conscience was clear, but she wanted me to understand that she in no way concurred in my reasons for keeping the flies out. She talked to herself for an hour after I left her: "Dat little no count fly can gi' you de typhoid fever! Lord, you is know dat I ain' tink nothin' like dat; I know dat You is de one dat send de trials and de tribulations o' dis world; 'tain't no little house-fly neither!"

❧

The mocking bird who lives with us and prefers us to the country, selecting the tallest chimney pot as a vantage point to shower down his repertoire culled from here and there and improved upon, proudly sends back the songs he has borrowed from lesser musicians, telling all the world how a bird should really sing. If I were as receptive as the mocking bird, I would have many a theme song on Charleston, for my work brings me in touch with so many phases of the city's life. There are infinite variations to be woven into the symphony which is Charleston, for the tongues of many lands have blended here.

No one predominant group could have given the flavor; it is a blend long mellowed by time. Music—suave manners —wit and humor—a love of beauty—epicurean tastes—soft voices—a fearless lack of hypocrisy and an easy tolerance, are contributions thrown into the pot which has had time to simmer long enough for the whole brew to become mysteriously seasoned with that elusive flavor—charm.

The city has had time with each new influx to absorb it slowly and gently, and not enough time to permit stagnation or provincialism. Changes are going on now, but the city is old, its standards well established; the pot is still brewing.

❧

This slower measure which we tread has brought many to visit us who have run the race too rapidly. They come to rest; we have something new for their eyes to see. They have heard rumors from their friends who have chanced in, of an old city still left with high walls and gardens barely visible through wrought-iron gates, of houses with plum-colored roofs and side piazzas entered from the street by

The Dock Street Theatre

doors crowned with fan lights. In the spring-time these visitors flit like butterflies through our streets, and the old city smiles a welcome.

If you like to study human vagaries, these transient visitors give you plenty of opportunities, for all types, classes and conditions are here. From every state in the Union they come. Charleston in the spring has more than she can easily handle, and every studio and shop is suitable for a laboratory. It is all so fleeting that it is hard when the city has settled back to regular living in May to remember them. A few each year stand out; quite a proportion of them are distinguished, and so many of them are charming. Most of them are in a very great hurry. I often wonder why they are so eager to see everything and thereby defeat their purpose and see so little.

They all ask where Catfish Row is, and it is so hard to explain that it is not really anywhere, when they have come so far to see it. DuBose Heyward had in mind a shabby double-house on Church street with an arch underneath it, but it suited his story best to put the house on the waterfront. The shabby house is far from shabby now. It is an apartment house with a pretty garden visible through the arch and the grill of the iron gate. It is hard to visualize it as the dwelling place of Porgy and Bess, and is harder still to tell every tourist who comes to town all of this.

Then the next question they ask is why the Sword Gates are so named. Because swords are in the pattern and spears, too, you explain; but that is not enough. *Why* are swords in the pattern?

They are likely to explain that Charleston is a most

unusual place and that we who live here should realize it and do something to preserve it. We tell them the story of the Dock Street Theatre, that masterpiece of restoration, combining as it does the lovely shell of one old building and the function of an earlier one. We ask them if they have visited the Heyward-Washington house, which is trying to forget its days of humiliation before it was rescued from the sale of penny gunja cakes, and now proudly recalls its days of glory when it entertained the First President.

That leads easily to Lafayette. Did he really speak to the people of Charleston from the balcony across the street? I can only assure them that I did not hear him, and so I cannot be too certain that he did. "But he may have," I add, when I see how disappointed they are.

What does it matter really? There is so much to see and to feel that by looking so hard at a point here or there, one loses the big design. Rather better to loiter along the streets than to rush hither and yon, to see this or that. Catch the tempo of the town. The beat is slower than the visitor has been accustomed to. Slow your hurrying feet; move to the rhythm of the *Moonlight Sonata*. Do not jazz it and do not explain to Charlestonians that all the world is jazzing it. We know that very well.

If you are weary of the syncopated unrest of a crazy world, come here and set your feet to a saner tempo. "What will we gain by that?" you ask. "All we'd accomplish would be to get out of step with the rest of the world." Perhaps that is so. We do not argue the point, but if you would only do it for a bit, there would be no need for argument, and you would leave us wiser than when you came. For the streets of Charleston have something to give those who walk them in a receptive mood that will make life forever richer.

❧

The green mold appliquéd by time on a rose brick wall makes that brick more than building material. As the cool lavender shadows and the warm yellow sunlight, patterned because of the narrow streets, play upon the rose and green of the old wall, a tapestry appears. The rose of the brick is mellowed by the opposing green. The result surprises the visitor. Green mold has become the alchemy that has wrought this harmony, green mold nurtured by time. A peace steals into one's heart, for green mold comes only where things endure. Through the centuries the city has endured—what deeds of valor, sacrifice and patient toil have gone into its making. What vicissitude it has suffered! The very bricks have become saturated with the emanations of heroism.

No Jamestown this, with monument to mark the spot, no Williamsburg resurrected, no Plymouth Rock to tax the imagination to visualize the landing of the Pilgrims; no Manhattan remains of the days of old Silver Leg. There is not a remnant left to help us picture the scene.

Here that green mold and those tiny ferns caught in the crevices of the brick help to bring back the days of the struggle. Right here this scene took place; right here these transplanted peoples from many lands started building a better world than the one that they had left, bringing with them memories which they wanted to keep of fair countries across the sea, and ideals for living which they could not make work there. They wanted all the best of what they had left and liberty besides.

For over two hundred and fifty years they have fought for just this. There is a continuity about it—a vision once caught and never forgotten—of what really counts in life.

It is the one colonial city in America with a living record which tells us, more vividly than all the books and all the old prints in museums can ever tell, what the new world inherited from the civilization of the ages. We started again, not to destroy the old law, but to fulfill it. Here the land is speaking—put your ear to the ground and listen.

Man's struggle for better living from the cave-dwellers on through the eons of time had reached a high point by the time America was founded. Materials for building had been evolved that were enduring and beautiful. Man had gone a long way from his remote arboreal ancestor when he was baking such beauty into that brick and turning the delicate tendrils in that cunningly wrought iron gate.

None of this skill was left overseas as unnecessary and unimportant. It was the heritage of the immigrant, and he would go on with what he had gained and add to man's triumph by justifying the struggle of the centuries.

The same instinct that made primitive man decorate his spearhead was demanding of these early settlers more than utility. The dignity of the human race is shown in those scrolls of iron—man's need to make beautiful the place where he lives.

So take your stroll along the narrow streets and realize that here in Charleston, America has remaining one city which has conserved more than a vestige of what was

St. John's Lutheran Church and The Unitarian Church

transplanted. Perhaps the stroll will clear things up and give a better sense of values.

Has the hurry to see more and to do more and to "get somewhere" after all been worth while? Very few have ever really "got" anywhere, for very few know where they want to get. Our Declaration of Independence, on which the ideals of America's freedom was founded, mentions life, liberty and the pursuit of happiness. These seem very simple aims to the average ambitious American who is rushing to get somewhere. To my mind Charleston realizes all three of these ultimate aims. Perhaps that is why people think us so slow. What is the use of hurrying when one is where one wants to be?

~

Elijah Green is the only person whom I know who really is completely satisfied. None of the famous people I have known have remotely approached the goal they set for themselves; all the wealthy ones long ago realized the limitations of money. But Elijah has his heart's desire. He dreamed as a little boy of being Charleston's oldest citizen, and he has attained his goal. He has no one left to disprove a detail of a single yarn, and he has lived to triumph over all his contemporaries. For Elijah is now one hundred and three years old; he can quote you a dozen passages in Holy Writ which promise long life to the just, and his conscience is clear as crystal. He has proved his justice to the Almighty and to himself, and all he has left to do is to prove it to us lesser beings who now inhabit the earth. To Elijah we are all an inferior breed. We did not live in the Golden Days;

we've only heard of them and read of them, whereas "I *know,* 'cause I been there!" is an argument that wins every time.

And who is left to say exactly what route Calhoun's funeral procession took from Canal Street to St. Philip's churchyard; who but Elijah. And who is there to refute his emphatic assertion that he helped to dig the grave of the great "John C. Caldwell Calhoun"? It seems improbable that any twelve or thirteen-year-old boy was given such an honor, but when he tells that his master bought him his first new shoes for the occasion, and that the great magnolia which keeps guard over the tomb was a small switch planted that day and that he helped to dig the hole for it, and that all the city was having holiday "as Mr. Zacharias Taylor done come down fum Washington, D.C.,"—he is very convincing.

He loves to measure his rise in life from that day as a little colored boy at the funeral of Carolina's greatest states-man and see how far he has come. He, of all that company, is left, so he, of all that company, is greatest in the sight of the Lord. Such utter satisfaction I have never witnessed in any other human being. That he was present also when "Ginrul Lee is give his sword to Useless Grant," and that he stood on the Battery and watched the bombardment, are among his lesser anecdotes. When I asked about the earth-quake of '86, he was insulted. "Why that jist yestidy, missus," he said, "better let me tell you bout de big fire of '61,—that was somethin' to remember."

I find profit in the little memory notes that he lets fall, the pictures he brings of the city that he knew as a boy. He has seen great changes in the city—both in her appear-ance and in her social life—but he will be quick to tell you

Side Piazzas

that it is the same old Charleston, because he knows, as do all of us know who live here, that the thing that makes us loyal to her is unchangeable.

❧

I have asked many persons what this permanent quality is that withstands changing conditions and, in the face of everything, keeps this strong appeal, and I think that the truest answer I have got so far is one a naval officer gave me not long ago.

He was not an analyst; he had never questioned in his long life away from Charleston that anyone would think it strange that he would want to come back after his time of service was over and end his life right here. He had, of necessity, traveled widely and seen many fair lands, but they were not for him.

"Why do I love it?" he asked and laughed. Such a foolish question, but I probed a little deeper. Not a foolish question, really—I wanted to know.

"Well," he told me at last after pondering deeply, "it's home."

And then I was satisfied,—*home!* What a beautiful word! Not perfect, but easy to live in; comfortable. For Charleston is no "period" city, as no house is a home that sets one date throughout. It is easy to walk into the living room of any house and see at a glance whether it is a home or the product of an interior decorator who knows all the answers but the one that matters. A home must reflect the personality of a family for many generations. It is a repository of treasure, not necessarily of any intrinsic value. A Morris chair is not a thing of beauty in itself, but, when a Morris chair has been the favorite chair of a beloved grandfather, it may be quite a suitable part of the library furniture. A clock which has been wound day in and day out for a lifetime is treasured beyond a better model in a museum. Here is a living record, the accumulation of mute witnesses of a family life.

Charleston is home to her children, because she satisfies this human craving. We may want to see the rest of the world change, but we would keep our homes exactly the way we are accustomed to thinking of them. There is no effort in the home; it is a place to relax and to be oneself— no pretense, absolute freedom, utter abandon.

We move so swiftly from one age to another. We are children—adolescent, adult and, before we have grasped it, middle-aged. On we go a little longer and it is all over for us. Life is so transient that all the while we would stay the ruthless swiftness of time. This is as instinctive as self-preservation, which is the first law of nature. It *is* self-preservation that we should try to stem the rushing tide and live a while before it is all over. This naval officer felt that way when he said that Charleston was home. Among his associates how few could retire to the city of their birth and call it home as he could and as his grandfather could have before him?

And is that not something to be proud of, or if not proud of, at least to be grateful for? We think so.

Nothing is more erroneous than the popular notion of a residential line in Charleston. "Below Broad Street" to the uninitiated has a smug sound, almost the sound "South of Market" has in Philadelphia. Of course this is all nonsense as all Charlestonians know, but it is one of those fallacies with which we have to contend. General Pershing has repeatedly denied that he was the one who said, "Lafayette, we are here," but has it ever registered? Above and below Broad Street are not different worlds in Charleston.

Many of Charleston's handsomest residences are above Broad Street, some of them still occupied by descendants of the original owners. However, in the difficult days following the War Between the States many families who lived up town moved down because they found it easier to be within walking distance of their friends since they had had to give up their carriages. Until comparatively recent years the upper part of the city still had low spots of marsh land, so the residences were farther apart. As the city grew and this low ground was filled in, the new land was taken over for new dwellings and business, leaving the old uptown residences at rather a disadvantage. Some so loved their old homes that they continued to stay there, but others moved down to the section of the city which had succeeded, for the most part, in remaining residential. Nothing could be more ridiculous than the assertion that where you live matters. If that were the criterion Charleston would be no different from a restricted residential park outside one of our Northern cities. It would certainly not be worth writing about. No one small neighborhood or social group would be that worth while; it would become ingrown, stupid and entirely uninteresting.

There is no north or south of Broad Street in Charleston

as I see it. The spirit of loyalty, humor and, above all, courtesy is a part of the body politic; it pervades the whole city, from the humblest Negro to our most distinguished citizen.

The politeness of our police force is in no little way responsible for our being able to retain this quality. It will be hard to credit in some places, but on one occasion I had an experience which I have told to other Charlestonians only to have them recount similar experiences of their own.

The black gloves ordered hastily over the telephone were too small; my friend asked that I exchange them as quickly as possible, for the funeral of a member of the family was only an hour distant when the error was discovered. I found no place to park my car, either in a parkway or on King Street, and so, risking a ticket for breaking the law, I stopped on the wrong side of the narrow street in front of our largest department store. I was about to leave the car when an officer came up and assured me that I could not park there. I explained my dilemma, and his sympathies were immediately aroused.

"What size do you want?" he asked. I told him and he went in and exchanged the gloves for me himself.

Early one morning my daughter and I were driving out of Charleston. Just as we passed the city line we had a blow-out. We were in despair, but not for long. A shifting engine stopped; the engineer got off and came to our rescue. "I'm always glad to help out a rival," he said. In no time our spare was on and we were on our way!

This could not happen many places, for time is too expensive to be given so lavishly, even to a rival.

St. Philip's Church

Sketching on the streets as I do, I hear so many things that escape the usual citizen. A retort I heard one day is remembered because it was the exception to this general rule of politeness. The Negroes are prone to salute each other in passing with a sort of caressing tenderness, and so, when I heard "Well, darlin', how is you feelin' today?" in a rich, deep voice, I was struck with the unusual response. "I feel like I choose," was the noncommittal rejoinder. How wonderful to be able to say, "I feel like I choose"! Who has not wanted to at some time?

Again I heard frankly expressed an opinion generally politely concealed, "Dat's we preacher tinnin' dat dere roof up yonder."

"Oh yes? *We* preacher don't do no wuk in de week," was her friend's complacent comment.

"How?" uttered with scorn. "You all is s'port a able-body man all de week? Gal, you is silly." And a laugh from both.

"Sammy," I heard whispered behind me one day when I was sketching, "what you tink dat lady is writin' dat picture wid?"

"She is writin' wid a pencil, can't you see?" was the answer.

"No, dat ain't no pencil, boy; it look like a pencil but it ain't, 'cause I got a pencil to my own house and it can't write nothin' like dat!"

Time and again I have suspected a street fight only to find it was a pleasant wrestling match. Once a street fight did develop too close for comfort when a friend and I were sketching. When it was all over the policeman who broke it up came and told us that the scuffle had been over the problem of which was "writin' " the best picture—the fair lady or the dark lady. I was the dark lady!

This same friend and I were interrupted another day with a request from a little girl, "Please ma'm, Ma say is when you all get trough wit your paintin' please to come down to de oyster fact'ry and paint de baby for she."

Do-As-You-Choose Alley appealed to me to etch. It is no more picturesque than a dozen other alleys, but somehow the name caught my fancy. The official name is Pearlstine Alley, but it is never called that, even in the police records. It was through the many times that it was mentioned as a locus of misdemeanors in the police records that I knew of it at all. The keeper of the jail directed me to the place. He said he knew it all too well, and that it was appropriately named.

As I parked my car squarely in front of the alley, for it was too narrow for traffic, I heard the man sitting indolently on the rickety step nearby say to the woman standing opposite with arms akimbo, "Susie, I is hear where yo' best fren is gone on de chain-gang yestiddy." I looked at Susie. She didn't deny the friendship; her facial expression never changed.

"Yes, I done hear 'bout dat myself," was her calm rejoinder. Imagine not changing expression on hearing your best friend had gone on the chain gang *yestiddy!*

An hour later a little girl timidly stepped up on the running board of my car. "Missus, can I see what you is writin' down on dat dey tin?" she asked.

"Yes," I answered, tilting the gleaming copper so she could see the lines into which I had rubbed a little ink. She was immediately excited and called her playmates.

"You all come see; de lady is write Mr. Manigault down for de life." Mr. Manigault was the stooped old figure supported by a walking stick whom I had sketched in as he slowly shuffled down the alley.

∾

The more distinguished the name in Charleston, the oftener it is encountered in the humbler strata. One picks up the paper in the morning and is shocked to read that Harriott Pinckney Prioleau Porcher, or some other hauntingly familiar combination, has died. One begins to wonder exactly who this can be, when on reading further, the funeral parlor and the burial ground clear up the mystery.

Washington is a favorite name. Perhaps many adopted it because they like the sound, and some may be the descendants of the people owned by Col. William Washington, who lived in Charleston. When sketching a cabin in the country not long ago, I asked the man hoeing a vegetable patch nearby, who lived in the cabin; he said that he did. I asked him his name. "Washington, missus," he replied. Just out of curiosity, I asked him what his other name was. "George," was his laconic reply.

"That's a very distinguished name you have, George," I said.

"Yes, ma'm?" he said. Nothing more. I wondered if he had ever heard of a better known George. I was not sure.

∾

One of the most interesting things about Charleston is our characters. I used to be afraid that they would all die out, for most of them were quite old. But they haven't. Just as soon as one goes and we all say the city will never be quite the same again, another starts sprouting eccentricities and filling in the breach. It would be impossible to describe any of them, for they are all so definitely themselves that their portraits would be too easily recognizable. The great difficulty in writing about any one particular locality is the danger of being too general in dealing with the subject to really paint a picture of it at all, or in being too specific, which might offend. I face the Scylla of deadly generalities or the Charybdis of becoming that obnoxious thing in any community—an intimate recorder of its foibles. It is like sketching on the streets, drawing your model off-guard, or like taking a snapshot of someone who prefers not to be photographed. Our privacy is an inherent right, and I have no intention of opening any closets or exposing any skeletons. There are reservations which all should respect, and besides, the secrets are irrelevant. They have nothing whatever to do with this illusive charm that I have been trying to convey.

All communities have their scandals, but all too few have retained the aroma of by-gone days in this changing world as has Charleston. Rather would I open a chest and get a whiff of jasmine long since laid there with treasure worth keeping, than a whiff of unwashed linen.

Charleston delights in her characters—their utter disregard for the conventional, their determination to live as they please, to act as they please and to dress as they please. There is little of the stereotyped anywhere. Not only do we have our outstanding eccentrics, but every group is composed of sharply drawn individuals. Charleston is rife with stories

Heyward-Washington House and Cabbage Row

about them; there is always the hope that, if one lives long enough and is courageous enough, one may some day be considered one of Charleston's characters.

The lady who lay in bed for forty years because she refused ever to get up again when she got the news of her lover's death in battle, has long since joined him, we hope, in a better world that knows no war.

And then there was our proud Gibson girl, who never changed her mode of dress from the Floradora days until she died not so long ago. Many an old trunk and chest was rummaged through by unknown friends to assist in this wardrobe. Outside her attic door she would find bundles of clothes surreptitiously placed, with tiny waists, full gored skirts, high-boned collars and petticoats with ruffles. It was rumored that her pompadour and her hat were inseparable, but no one ever really knew, for no one ever knew her quite that well. She was the most difficult person to assist Charleston ever had!

She did not fit into any of our institutions, for there she made all the other ladies uncomfortable by telling them how much better she was than they were. She would attend one church, then another, and work up a whole congregation into a crescendo of pity for her plight and then scorn any assistance offered her. She did not hesitate to remark quite audibly that the sermon was entirely too long, if she thought so.

There are a hundred stories about her refusals to be helped; the whole town knew she was starving, but her pride was her impregnable armour; no one could ever find a way to pierce it. Charleston's charitable organizations used all the strategy possible, but she sensed pity from afar and drew away with scorn into her lonely garret. All she had left in the world was her pride. She must not lose her only possession; the conspiracy to save it for her was carefully observed by the whole city.

And then, too, Charleston had for many years a self-imposed ambassador of good will. He spent his latter days in circling the globe and calling on exiled Charlestonians in out-of-the-way places, giving them the news and bringing home messages to their families. The places that he visited interested him not at all. If he felt energetic he would land for an hour or two and buy post cards to send back to his Charleston friends and seek a newspaper office to let it be known that a Charlestonian was in port, and then he would go back to his ship and check up on his Charleston list to see who was next.

When he was taken seriously ill on one of these voyages on the other side of the world, he instructed the captain of the ship to get in touch with Charlestonians at the next port of call, feeling sure that he would be taken care of, which of course he was, for they never deserted him, and when a few days later he died, they sent him back on his last trip to Charleston.

The little lady with the bobbing curls who would not change her coiffure for reasons of sentiment has also left us, and, too, the lady who forever hid behind a veil. These and the collar-button gentleman and so very many others have gone, but there are so many left that the result is practically the same. Every town has these individuals who refuse to follow the conventional pattern. They are called

St. Matthew's Church from Marion Square

freaks in some places, eccentrics in others, but we like them and humor them. I would almost say we encourage them. They give variety and spice. The salt would lose its savor if Charleston were to lose too many of these interesting people at one time. The city has escaped the standardization of personality which has made so many communities dull.

They cannot be called types and pigeonholed, for each is so individual and unpredictable that one can not ever say, "She is a perfect Mrs. Jellaby," or he, a Micawber. Dickens would have delighted in them, but he never met their counterpart in London. They are a product of this particular city, and nowhere else on earth. After all, why should we follow like sheep? If we do not break the code, which is gentility and breeding, there seems no reason why we should not all live in Do-As-You-Choose Alley.

❧

It is unfortunate that we are never wholly ourselves in springtime, when Charleston is loveliest and the world visits us. We try to be, but it is very hard. Our visitors come with a preconceived idea of what Charleston is and what Charleston stands for. For the most part they have a very good impression of us. We try not to let them down. Though perhaps their visit is too fleeting for them to get a glimpse of that inner Charleston, they seem to find so much to admire that they come back and send their friends. They delight in the glimpses of the gardens in full bloom when theirs are still covered with snow, the multi-colored plastered walls and the narrow streets. They are amused by the hucksters' calls and try to coax reluctant flower women to stand long enough for a snapshot. They enjoy poking around in our old churchyards and reading quaint epitaphs. They sense the very things we cannot express at the moment, because these are so deeply rooted in the city itself that they speak for themselves. So, in spite of the failure of the actors, the stage setting carries the drama.

All through the lovely spring days they come, from the blooming of the first azalea in February when the camellia is still in its glory, until the dogwood tree has turned from white to apple-green, and then one morning they are gone, as the swallows go. It is so sudden that we are dazed by the swift change. The day before we have hung on the telephone trying to find some place for a friend to sleep and the next day the city is quiet; the rush is over for another year. The azaleas have gone, too, but the beauty of the city is just beginning. The oleander is about to bloom, and the great buds on the *Magnolia grandiflora* are slowly opening. The bignonia is bordering the tops of our walls with gold, and the tiny chicken shrimp are coming in. Soon we shall have figs again.

We are beginning to wish that we could have done more for this and that charming person who has left too soon— we are becoming very normal. Perhaps we realize then why we are a different people; there is no mystery in it, for we are exactly like every one else when we have been faced by the conditions that most of the world live under all the time, and we have handled the situation neither better nor worse than it is handled elsewhere. If we lived in the busy marts of the world, we would be like the people who live there; that is proved in the springtime, when for a month Charleston is a busy city.

If these visitors stopped with us longer they, too, would find that they have time to live as we live. And so we are not so very different, after all. It is the city that is different.

Very soon the beautiful month of May with its flowers is over, and the long, hot days begin. At first they seem bearable. We strip our houses of all unnecessary draperies, install cool matting rugs and electric fans. It is so pleasant still that no one wishes to leave, but the long, long days are ahead. School is over and so the city thins out; one by one the houses are closed. Off most of us go to the beaches and the mountains.

The old city sleeps. The few that stay at home know how to take it. The heavy shutters are hooked in to keep out the glare and heat. Shopping is done early, or late in the afternoon; no one hurries. There are no sunstrokes; the gentle breezes from the sea bring relief, and when it all seems too unbearable, a blessed roll of thunder is heard. Quick vivid zigzags of lightning follow and a tropical storm brings respite for awhile.

It is in weary September that the city reaches low tide; even the flagstones which pave the streets never lose their heat. All day long they absorb, and all the weary night they throw it off. The city is listless and very, very tired. It is hard to realize then that October is only a few weeks ahead.

October in Charleston is what spring must be in Alaska. It comes so suddenly it is like cool spring water to a throat-parched traveller. It has always seemed to me that our Sundays through the fall and winter are especially beautiful. Little yellow butterflies flit here and there; people promenade for the sheer joy of it along the high Battery. The water in the quiet harbor is blue as it has not been all summer. Friend greets friend.

The fall is long, lasting often up to Christmas. The flower women bring in zinnias with the goldenrod and that lovely spiked purple weed well after Thanksgiving. Roses bloom on until it freezes. We know it does freeze in Charleston but we do not like to face it until we have to. Not long at a time, ever. When we have turned off the water pipes and are grimly determined to make the best of it, the sun comes out, and it is all over. It seldom, very seldom, snows. We are too close to the sea for that. Even in January tiny signs that it is nearly over are evidenced, and by February, we are well on the way to spring again. A long spring and a longer fall; that is the way we think of Charleston. When the air is cool in the shade and warm in the sun and a gentle sea breeze is blowing, we will tell you that it is a typical Charleston day. We are positively embarrassed by too much cold or too much rain, for we feel quite responsible, and no matter how often it happens it is always "most unusual." It is like having a dearly beloved member of the family in a bad humor.

The city belongs personally to every one of us. For many years now I have been seeking the reason for this devotion. In the Orient, with my spine at ease in the familiar curves of a Charleston rocking chair before a coal grate fire, with the sounds of the East coming in through the window, I have asked the question. Almost it was answered for me without words by the portrait of a Carolina gentleman over the mantel in dull gold frame, which had crossed the wide Pacific to act as hall mark for his children in exile.

The Sword Gates

I have asked it, teacup in hand, in a Paris drawing room with the sound of Charleston voices about me. I have asked it at random of students, porters on trains, diplomats and laundresses. I have asked it of high and low, wherever I have met a Charlestonian away from home. Always they seem surprised that I ask it. The answer seems so obvious it would be banal to analyze. Of course they love Charleston better than any place on earth—of course—but again I reiterate, why?

Why does the smell of pluff mud and fertilizer plants seem aromatic to our nostrils? Why does the salt flatness of artesian water quench our thirst? Why do houses on narrow streets with no place to park seem preferable to boulevards? Why do we enjoy being awakened before time by the raucous, unintelligible jargon of a shrimp vender? We are perfectly aware that life is not ideal here; we know our frailties better than we would have the world know that we know them. We are constantly telling each other how shocking this condition is and that. We are not as complacent as we would have outsiders believe.

With it all, however, we do insist that we have harbored here a secret ally that has become for most of the world a ruthless foe. We have made a friend of Time in Charleston.

Yes, as Rebecca remarked, "Chas'n don't change none and it keep all de odder place on earth from seem natchel."